1986 edition published by Greenwich House,
distributed by Crown Publishers, Inc.
ISBN 0 517 62281 5
h g f e d c b a
Dep. Leg. B-27.308-86

Invitation to a
ROYAL WEDDING

Text by Trevor Hall

Foreword by

Michael Mayne, Dean of Westminster

Introduction by

Miles, Duke of Norfolk, Earl Marshall of England

GREENWICH HOUSE

The photographs in this book will remind you of a day of royal splendour, and bring back some of the beauty of colour and sound which made this wedding, in the incomparable setting of Westminster Abbey, an occasion to lift the heart.

Although millions were watching on television, those of us who took part were chiefly concerned to make the marriage service a memorable and even intimate event in the lives of the two people who were at the centre of it.

As it happened, I was installed as Dean of Westminster between two weddings which, in different ways, were of great significance to me. The previous week, in my church in Cambridge, I officiated at the wedding of my own daughter – also Sarah – and shared the joy of two people, deeply in love, making a lifelong commitment to each other.

The setting of that wedding, and that of the Royal Wedding a fortnight after my installation, could not have been more different. But at the heart of each event were the same words, the same emotions, and the same joy of two separate people beginning the mysterious process of becoming what the Bible calls 'one flesh'.

To believe in marriage is to believe that a man and a woman can commit themselves in a lifelong relationship of unconditional love. They make promises which are binding, and each accepts responsibility for the other, in good days and bad – a commitment strong enough to survive the occasional rows and misunderstandings which are part of the long process of growing together.

The relationship can be enormously difficult, but where it succeeds it is uniquely rewarding. It calls for openness, for absolute trust and loyalty, and not least for a mutual cherishing and encouragement of each other. It calls for a quality of love which, in St Paul's words, 'is always patient... which does not take offence, is not resentful... and is always ready to excuse, to trust, to hope and to endure'.

For each to say to the other, within the trusting security of marriage, *I give myself to you unconditionally* does not diminish them as individuals, but enhances them, for in marriage we complement each other and, in a mysterious way, need each other to become our true selves.

Every wedding witnesses to this vision of the love between two people creating that which is new and life-giving; a setting in which children can grow and flourish. It gives us something to celebrate. At a Royal Wedding we celebrate the same truth, but on an infinitely larger canvas.

Michael Mayne

Michael Mayne
Dean of Westminster

Introduction

It is interesting to reflect that, of the twelve countries comprising the European Economic Community, six are happily ruled by Kings, Queens or, in one case, by a reigning Grand Duke. Their political structures are in fact constitutional monarchies, where the monarch is head of state but with little direct political power. We in Britain have evolved this excellent form of government since the Revolution of 1688, and now our Queen plays a considerable part in ruling her United Kingdom (and, indeed, the Commonwealth) where her rights have been so well described by Bagehot as 'to be consulted, to encourage and to warn'.

It cannot go unnoticed that the republican countries of Europe greatly envy us our continuing royal heritage. Indeed, they so often proudly refer to their own history by highlighting the deeds and reigns of *their* powerful kings, such as Louis XIV of France. Perhaps the greatest hero in French history was Napoleon I, whom Frenchmen idolise as their Emperor – even though he was born in Corsica and, starting as a young artillery officer, grew to power through various *coups d'état*. How comparatively tawdry and dull are the trappings that surround a president of a republic against the splendour and royal traditions of a monarchy, and how lucky we are to have a Royal Family which remains united and whose every family event, such as this memorable wedding of Prince Andrew and Miss Sarah Ferguson, becomes an occasion of national rejoicing and happiness.

Many people think that the Earl Marshal is responsible for the ceremonial of royal marriages, but this is not the case: he has not organised royal weddings since the days of Queen Anne. Subsequent weddings have been the responsibility of the Lord Chamberlain because Georgian and Victorian weddings of the Royal Family usually took place inside the royal palaces themselves. This reflects the division of responsibility of the medieval Officers of the Court. The Earl Marshal's was originally a military role, and he is therefore still responsible for some of the external ceremonial activities of the monarch – State occasions such as the Investiture of the Prince of Wales at Caernarfon Castle, the Opening of Parliament, the funeral of Sir Winston Churchill and, of course the greatest of all State occasions, the Coronation of the Sovereign. Broadly speaking, the Lord Chamberlain looks after the other activities of the Sovereign, the royal palaces and the organisation of events within their walls. By implication, this essentially private royal wedding is one of those events.

Finally, we Yorkshiremen rejoice in all the popular clamour for the creation of Prince Andrew as Duke of York – a title taken from the second city of England, ranking immediately after London as one of the few cities which have a Lord Mayor. And York's coat of arms, so simple and so historic with its red cross of St George and the lions of the Plantagenet kings, bears ample witness to our royal heritage.

I am delighted to have had this opportunity to set down these few thoughts to introduce this colourful and informative book to you. I am sure that, as you turn its pages, you will enjoy its lively text and brilliant illustrations, and will come to value it for many years as a superb, lasting memento of a glorious day in the life of our Royal Family.

Miles, Duke of Norfolk
Earl Marshal of England

'I've got to get used to this "we" business!' exclaimed Prince Andrew, with his usual broad grin and happy-go-lucky chuckle. But there was a defensiveness in his smile, for he had just made – and not for the first time that morning – the cardinal mistake of referring to himself when he should have been referring to himself and his new fiancée. And his fiancée was sitting next to him.

They were talking about wedding plans, and he, after twenty-six years of being very much his own man, was being elbowed in the ribs every time he said 'I' when he should have said 'we'. And the lady responsible for the elbowing was determined to remind him in that way

Only in the sense that the conversation was taking place at Buckingham Palace could Prince Andrew consider himself to be on home ground. Had he been almost any other British mortal, he could that day have announced his engagement and simply proceeded to accomplish the business of a normal day. But as a prince of the blood royal and fourth in line to the throne of a thousand years, he now found himself confronting a succession of press, radio and television interviewers, facing a barrage of questions about when, where and why the engagement had taken place at all, and what his (sorry, their) plans were for the immediate and long term future.

that, behind her own ready and irrepressible smile, it was 'we' from now on. Not the royal 'we' of course, for that went out of fashion long ago, except for official proclamations and Acts of Parliament, but the matrimonial 'we'. Right? Right!

When Sarah joined the Princess of Wales for a private visit to see Andrew on board his ship HMS Brazen in February 1986, the long-running rumours of an engagement between her and the Queen's second son seemed confirmed. (Opposite page and top) Andrew and Diana lead young Prince William round

the ship, while Sarah stays discreetly in the background. (Above) one of Sarah's first official appearances after her engagement: helping to collect thousands of daffodils brought by children to Buckingham Palace to celebrate the Queen's 60th birthday.

Horse laughs: Andrew and Sarah's pleasant Spring afternoon at the Windsor Horse Show, just a short drive away from Windsor Castle. Royalty rarely relaxes more fully than when surrounded by horses, and Sarah's reactions to the day's thrills and spills made it evident that she is very much at home sharing the Royal Family's favourite fascination.

At first glance, it should not have been too difficult for someone already well accustomed to fielding interviewers' enquiries. But, like most royals who have submitted themselves to media scrutiny, Prince Andrew has always chosen to answer questions on subjects on which he might be described as an authority.

enjoying it all as a child enjoys its first outing to a funfair. Sitting straight-backed in the soft immensity of one of Buckingham Palace's less distinguished sofas (part of the furniture of Prince Andrew's suite of rooms), she parried the ammunition fired at her by her inquisitors, chipped in where Prince Andrew

faltered, giggled and fooled around as if unaware that on this of all occasions she would be heard and seen round the world, and generally gave the unmistakable impression that she was having a whale of a time, secure in the knowledge that it was better to have arrived than merely to travel.

(Right) Sarah at the Clapham home she shared before her engagement. (Above) the spacious Ferguson family home, heart of an 800-acre farming estate in the tiny Hampshire village of Dummer.

Unfortunately, there were no questions about helicopters here, nor about photography, nor about Gordonstoun, nor about the Falklands conflict. He was here to talk about a major change in his life and lifestyle, a future of which he could be certain of precious little, and a wife-to-be who kept digging him in the ribs every time he said 'I' instead of 'we'. No wonder he was a touch uneasy.

She, by contrast – the Sarah Ferguson whose name had been in every newspaper with increasing frequency for the best part of a year – seemed to be

Unlike Prince Andrew, who could not, even on this day, get out of the entrenched royal habit of striving for circumspection while giving serious, comprehensive and well-considered answers to weightier matters, Sarah was entirely self-possessed throughout, apologising only once – and then with a mischievous self-mockery – for not being serious enough, and leading everybody, including her future husband, to believe that she had no intention of being left out.

Even before the interview began, the couple were noticeably more relaxed. 'Where's the make-up?' joked the Prince, and Sarah nudged him as her freckled face broadened into unaffected laughter. She was wearing a sharply tailored navy blue wool suit with a wrap-over front giving a double-breasted effect, and an expansive shoulder line that might even

Statistics for the 'Big Day'

Considering that even royal wedding ceremonies last only for an hour, the involvement of time, money and manpower is monumental. Television audiences world wide amount to over 750 million, almost a thousand times the number of spectators who line the route for a glimpse of the royal couple, and 400,000 times as many as the number of wedding guests. An army of florists, hairdressers, cosmeticians, valets and maids have to be up before daybreak to attend to bride and groom, rivalling for early rising another army of photographers, journalists, television cameramen and radio commentators all wrestling with sheafs of notes and hundreds of miles of cable in the half-light of dawn. Unsolicited wedding gifts number up to 10,000, of which about 3,000 are kept and a few hundred exhibited publicly. Among the gifts there are normally a good dozen wedding cakes, in addition to the official one measuring some four feet high, weighing between one and two hundredweight, and sufficient to feed over a thousand. But the wedding breakfast is comparatively modest: less than a hundred guests – closest family only. And only one toast, drunk in silence, with no speeches.

have made Princess Diana envious. The jacket was cinched in (as the jargon has it) above the waist by a deep, waist-hugging black belt, and complemented by an unpressed pleated skirt of spectacular length. Underneath the jacket she wore a simple, unadorned, round-necked blouse in vivid magenta crêpe-de-chine, while a matching ribbon bunched part of her huge mane of red hair. Sarah had bought the outfit only a couple of days before, from Alistair Blair, a 30-year-old up-and-coming fashion designer for whom Viscount Linley's girlfriend, Susannah Constantine, once worked as

Sarah in a supporting role as Andrew joins an annual celebrity clay pigeon shoot. (Opposite) well protected from the crack of gunfire. (Below right) helping Andrew and Jackie Stewart to celebrate at the end of the day.

an assistant. That same week, as it happened, Blair had received standing ovations for his creations at the London Fashion Week shows. Sarah looked more than pleased that she had, unwittingly, picked a winner.

Two television interviewers were confident that they, too, had picked their own winner. Before long, their conversation with Andrew and his new-found bride-to-be became delightfully casual, rather more revealing, and easily as enjoyable as any royal interview in the twenty-five years or so since Prince Philip became the subject of the first tentative and respectful step to involve royalty in public conversation. In less than twenty minutes, Andrew and Sarah showed just how far the art had come since then.

Question: Congratulations to you, Sir, and best wishes to both of you. Could you tell us, please, first of all, how long ago

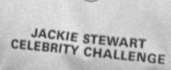

it was that you decided to marry?

Andrew: I asked Sarah some weeks ago, and Sarah actually said Yes, which...

Sarah: Surprising.

Andrew: ...surprised me. But she did say also... A little anecdote for you is that she said: 'If you wake up tomorrow morning you can tell me it's all a huge joke.' I didn't!

A quick kiss for Andrew and Sarah (above) on their engagement day. (Previous pages) Windsor, two months later: Sarah solitary and pensive; and animated with Andrew.

Sarah: So we're sitting here.

Question: So you started from a meeting at Ascot?

Andrew: Yes.

Question: And then everything developed from there in a way. When did you both know it was the real thing?

Andrew: Again, very difficult to answer, but I think that probably the end of last year, before Christmas, perhaps...

Sarah: Yes.

Andrew: And then it sort of...

Sarah: ...carried on from there.

Andrew: Carried on from there after Christmas at Sandringham, and then beyond that.

Question: What first impressions did you have of one another then, in that case?

Sarah: Very good friends.

Andrew: (a) Very good friends, and (b) it was at lunch – wasn't it? – that...

Sarah: Yes.

Andrew: ...we were made to sit next door to each other at Ascot.

Sarah: Yes, and he made me eat chocolate profiteroles, which I didn't want to eat at all.

Andrew: I then didn't have any. So I got hit.

Sarah: Very hard!

Andrew: And it started from there. I think that's probably where it...

Sarah: I was meant to be on a diet.

Question: And that was the basis of a romance?

Sarah: Yes.

Andrew: There are always humble beginnings. It's got to start somewhere. But, I mean, we've known each other since we were four or five – perhaps not knowingly since four or five – until, again, about 1983 when we were staying at various house parties together around the country during the part of '83 and '84, and it was at Ascot that, as it were, the whole thing, as you say, took off. And it wasn't at Ascot as such that we realised that there was anything in it. It was later on.

Sarah: Yes.

Question: I think you said, Sir, that when you met the right girl, it would probably come like a lightning bolt.

Andrew: You're not the first person who's asked me this question today. In fact there are about three or four other people who've asked it. And I'm really at a loss to say... I mean, I don't think that Sarah is a thunderbolt.

Sarah: Nor am I a streak of lightning. Nor is he, I don't think.

Question: Can I ask you if you can tell us what you like about each other?

Andrew: Oh!

Sarah: Wit. Charm.

Andrew: Yes, probably.

Sarah: Yes.

Andrew: And the red hair.

Sarah: And the good looks! (**Pulls a face, slaps Andrew on the leg, and laughs.**) Sorry!

Question: Could we...?

Andrew: I'm watching carefully! Go on.

Question: Could we perhaps now have a rather more lingering look at the ring? I mean, how did you find time to – or the secrecy, the away-from-the-media-ness – to go out and buy it?

Andrew: Well, very fortunately I didn't actually have to go out and buy. Somebody very kindly came in with some suggestions, and it was made very kindly by some very nice engineers, I think.

Sarah: Engineers?

Andrew: I don't think they'd like to be called engineers, but...

Sarah: Definitely not!

Andrew: ...I don't know what you'd call them.

Sarah: Jewellers!

Andrew: Jewellers.

Question: Miss Ferguson, how would you describe that lovely ring?

Sarah: Stunning. Red – I wanted a ruby. Well, I didn't want it – I'm very lucky to have it. But certainly it's a lovely stone. And I've got red hair too.

Andrew: It was... again, it's something that we discussed in the last few weeks, and

EAU CLAIRE DISTRICT

we came to the mutual conclusion that red was probably the best colour for Sarah. And that's how we came to the choice of the ruby. And then the extra bits round the outside – we wanted something that was slightly unconventional, and I think we've got something there.

Sarah: Yes, very original. I think Andrew – you actually designed it, didn't you?

Andrew: Er, I helped in the design.

Question: What, you mean with sketches and things?

Andrew: Well, we did sketch some of it, and I found a suggestion in another selection of rings that I was given, and then I asked them to check... I'm not quite sure what the shape of the original was that I drew, but they looked like rugby balls – little tiny ones – and these are drops rather than rugby balls.

Sarah: Thank goodness for that! I'd hate to wear a rugby ball round my hand.

Question: Can you tell us about the proposal – where and when it took place?

Andrew: It was some weeks ago, staying privately in Scotland. And I'd go no further than saying that.

Question: Could I ask you then, Miss Ferguson, do you remember what he said?

Sarah: Absolutely. But I'm not telling you!

Question: Did he go down on one knee in the approved fashion?

Andrew: No, both. That I will tell you. Both.

Sarah: Yes, both.

Question: And you, of course, very formally asked your prospective father-in-law for Miss Ferguson's hand in marriage?

Andrew: Yes, that was also fairly nerve-racking, knowing Major Ronald from a long time ago, at the polo. And I asked him this week-end, as well as Her Majesty.

Question: What was the Queen's reaction?

Andrew: Overjoyed. Very happy, very pleased. And beyond that, I think that – what else? – I mean, just as a delighted parent, I think.

Sarah: As indeed is my father.

Question: There was no phrase using the words 'settling down' when she said 'Congratulations'?

Profile

Name: Sarah Margaret Ferguson
Date of birth: October 15, 1959
Place of birth: London
Father: Major Ronald Ferguson
Mother: Mrs Susan Barrantes (formerly Ferguson, née Wright)
Sister: Jane, born 1957, married (to Alex Makin) with 1 daughter
Stepmother: Mrs Susan Ferguson
Half-brother and sisters: Andrew (7), Alice (5), Eliza (b. 1985)
Family Home: Dummer Down Farm, near Basingstoke, Hampshire
Schools: (1) Daneshill Prep School, Basingstoke; (2) Hurst Lodge, Sunningdale, Berkshire
Qualifications: 6 'O' Levels, 2 CSEs
Career: Worked for flat-letting agency; art dealer; sports PR agency; graphic arts company.
Height: 5' 9"
Colour of hair: Auburn-red
Colour of eyes: Hazel

Andrew: How do you mean, 'settling down'?

Question: Well, becoming a married man...

Andrew: Oh, Gosh! I see; that way.

Question: ...and responsibilities thereby.

Andrew: No, no. I mean, I don't see there's anything settling in it. It's a mighty upheaval for most people, and I think it'll be an upheaval for both of us in terms of we've both got to come to terms (a) with life as it will continue...

Sarah: We're a good team, anyway.

Andrew: Yes. I think that's the saving grace, the fact that in the last nine months we've discovered that we work very well together.

Sarah: We're good friends; a good team. Quite happy... very happy.

Question: Miss Ferguson, could I ask you, how do you think you're going to cope with this new role and at the same time being a Navy wife?

Sarah: I'm going to enjoy it immensely. I think I'm going to cope with the help of Andrew here.

Andrew: I think it's worth saying that I have no plans to change my Navy career, on the advice of Sarah.

Sarah: Very strongly.

Andrew: We discussed it at some length, and for the foreseeable future I will be continuing my naval career as it is at the moment. Sarah is quite prepared to put up with that, and I think that she will be a remarkable wife if she can. And I know how difficult it is – talking to naval colleagues of mine – what it's like to be married to a naval officer, because we do spend such a long time away.

Sarah: Also, I've got a job to do, too. And I'm going to keep on working, and... So I think it's going to be very good.

Question: You think it will be possible to keep on working...

Sarah: Absolutely.

Question: ...with the pressures that...

Sarah: Absolutely.

Question: ...tend to apply?

Sarah: My job is a printing and publishing job, therefore I have the freedom to... and

(Previous page and left) a stunning Sarah arrives for a charity theatre production at Weymouth in June. (Right) all smiles as the Andrew/Fergie engagement secret is out.

since I work for myself I have the freedom to, sort of, arrange things round what I can do. So I can do a bit of everything, really.

Andrew: I think it's a great advantage in being almost self-employed and working for somebody outside the country and running an office over here, in that Sarah's (a) her own boss here, so she can make her own work schedules up to suit herself, and she knows that there are times when she has to go to work, therefore she can go to work.

Sarah: Mmm. So when Andrew's away I will work harder than perhaps when Andrew's here. Right? Right.

Andrew: Hopefully.

Question: Have you, in the course of this rather difficult last month or so had any advice from the Prince and Princess of Wales, who went through much the same thing?

Sarah: The Princess of Wales and I are extremely good friends and we naturally talk about a lot of different subjects.

Question: Like dealing with the media?

At Royal Ascot (left) Sarah tried out a Texan-size fashion idea. She had already made famous the giant bow hair-ribbon (below) and sported the fly-away brim (below right) – a royal favourite.

Profile

Name: Andrew Albert Christian Edward Mountbatten-Windsor
Date of birth: February 19, 1960
Place of birth: Buckingham Palace
Father: HRH Prince Philip
Mother: HM Queen Elizabeth II
Brothers: (1) HRH The Prince of Wales; (2) HRH Prince Edward
Sister: HRH Princess Anne
Family homes: Windsor Castle, Buckingham Palace, Sandringham, Balmoral Castle Schools: Heatherdown Preparatory School, Berkshire; Gordonstoun; Lakefield College, Ontario
Qualifications: 6 'O' Levels, 3 'A' Levels
Career: Began 12-year Royal Navy commission in 1979 as helicopter pilot. Saw action in the Falklands and is now a Lieutenant
Height: 5' 11"
Colour of hair: Dark brown
Colour of eyes: Blue

Sarah: Lots of different subjects.

Andrew: Yes, I think that's possibly the best way of answering that. I mean, there...

Sarah: We're very, very good friends.

Andrew: ...there are so many different, differing ideas about how to handle yourself that you can't take one person's advice all the time.

Sarah: Although there is no-one better than the Princess of Wales.

Question: The plans for the wedding are by no means final – in fact, you don't even know when or where.

Andrew: No.

Question: What sort of wedding would you like to have?

Andrew: Er – as in red, white or blue? No. I hope a London wedding, and I hope a white wedding. Sarah is already charging around looking for a dress – or looking for ideas. Beyond that, I have absolutely no idea.

Sarah: You've got your dress?

Andrew: Yes, I've got my dress, thank you.

Yes. I'm not so sure that it would fit. But anyway, the plans are still up in the air because now of course we go on into the planning stage and the summer schedule is a very tight one, and I would very much like it to be in the summer – and so would Sarah. Sarah more so because I think that...

Sarah: Mmm – get on with it.

Andrew: Get on with it and get it out of the way. Because of course the summer schedule's very tight this year and I would hope some time perhaps in July or August. If it's not possible to do it in July or August, then I think...

Sarah: We would, yes.

Andrew: Sorry – we: I've got to get used to this 'we' business.

Sarah: I know, it's difficult, isn't it? We – OK?

Andrew: We. That's right.

Sarah: Right.

Andrew: Otherwise the fall-back is sometime in the autumn.

Question: It has been a bit of a whirlwind, hasn't it, really? You've only known each other for – what is it? – nine months?

Sarah: Definitely not!

Question: No?

Andrew: I certainly wouldn't consider it a whirlwind at all. It may be a whirlwind to some people because, of course, I suppose that the media only discovered about it in...

Sarah: In January.

Andrew: ...in January/December, just after Christmas, but...

Sarah: In fact, there's...

Andrew: ...there's quite a lot that went on before. In fact more than what went on after.

Question: What are your plans between now and the wedding?

Sarah: Hard work.

Andrew: Hard work. I've got a course to do.

Sarah: I've got a job to do.

Andrew: So we shall be getting on with it. The course that I'm going to do finishes as the beginning of June, so I will have the time to sit down and plan the wedding and the arrangements afterwards.

Question: Looking towards the future a little, you come from – both of you – from fairly large families. Would you like to repeat that pattern? Would you like to have quite a lot of children?

Andrew: I don't know really. I mean... (**To Sarah**) What do you say?

Sarah: Don't know. What do you say?

Andrew: I think that we haven't actually... I mean, that's something that – until we get married – that we haven't, sort of, thought about. There is an awful lot to think about in the next – whatever it is – until we get married.

Sarah: Quite fun to have quite a few, anyway.

Andrew: I agree, it would be quite fun.

But, again, number, size and all the rest of it is still way, way in the future, and really it's not possible...

Sarah: It has yet to be decided.

Question: Notionally, it's a good idea, though?

Andrew: Yes.

Question: Can I put a final question to you, Miss Ferguson? How do you feel about your new title, because after your marriage you'll be known as Princess Andrew?

Sarah: Umm...

Andrew: You can answer that one!

Sarah: I'm going to! How do I feel about my new title? Er – what's the word?

Andrew: Change of name?

Sarah: Change of name. A great honour. Much looking forward to carrying it out, whatever I'm supposed to do. That's it, I think.

Question: Do you think, in public terms, that they'll have rather a hard job getting

Despite their different backgrounds, the Fergusons are no strangers to the Windsors. There are distant blood ties, but more recently the Royal Family's interest in polo brought them together over twenty years ago.

all the way from Fergie to Princess Andrew?

Sarah: No.

Question: I mean, you've caught the affection over the past few months as Fergie: suddenly Princess Andrew seems a bit of a mouthful.

Andrew: It's not all that sudden. You have got time to acclimatise to it. I mean, we are talking of some months away.

Sarah: You could find a nickname around Princess Andrew!

Andrew: Mmm – yes, well all right... But I'm not going to help, though!

Question: May I, on behalf of ITN and the BBC, offer you our best wishes and all happiness for the future.

Andrew: Thank you very much.

Sarah: Thank you very much indeed.

With that, the biggest hurdle that life had thus far placed before Sarah Ferguson was successfully cleared. Like most stories in which the sort of everyday girl you would not particularly notice in a crowd is met, wooed and won by a prince, that morning's events were a far cry in time and circumstance from the early autumn day in 1959 when she first saw the light, if not of day, then of a delivery room at a nursing home in Welbeck Street in London's West End.

Sarah Margaret Ferguson was born on 15th October, 1959. At the time, and barely half a mile away, Her Majesty Queen Elizabeth II was in the fifth month of her third pregnancy – which would result in the birth of Prince Andrew the following February. Little did Sarah's parents suspect how significant the two events would turn out to be for both

Sarah enjoyed the Windsor Horse Show (previous pages), joined Andrew for polo in Royal Ascot week (these pages) and again to present the Queen's Cup at Windsor early in June (overleaf).

Prince Andrew does not play polo, but first met Sarah while watching a match in which both their fathers played at Smith's Lawn, Windsor Great Park, in 1965. Since Prince Charles took up the game, Andrew has been a frequent spectator – Sarah too, since her close friend Princess Diana first took an interest, and since her father became Vice Chairman of Guards Polo Club.

infants and their families.

There was little reason to put two and two together in those early days. Though the Fergusons can claim all manner of royal connections in their complex and sometimes quite aristocratic family tree, they were very much on the fringes of royal acquaintaince. Sarah's father, Major Ronald Ivor Ferguson, now retired from the Life Guards, once commanded the Sovereign's Escort of the Household Cavalry – they nicknamed him 'the General' as a result – and this had brought him into close contact with the Queen in the early years of her reign. He became the driving force behind (and is now Vice-Chairman of) Guards Polo Club, . the association which Prince Philip and later Prince Charles were to join, but the early personal ties between Windsors and Fergusons were at best tenuous.

For Ronald Ferguson, these were the prime years of family life. He had been married in his early twenties to Susan Wright, an attractive teenager with a personality which, though precociously strong, matched her husband's liking for straight talk and direct action. Despite the six years' difference in their ages, the marriage blossomed and within four years the couple were the parents of two daughters.

Sarah may have laughed and smiled on her engagement day, and (although from the few early family photographs so

Contrasts for a princess-to-be: Sarah cheerful and wind-blown (left) on a gusty May afternoon; and smart and sedate at Royal Ascot in sunny June.

far released publicly, and which show her as rather serious and self-effacing, apparently reluctant to be photographed at all, it might seem that this was not always so) she appears to have been laughing and smiling almost since the day of her birth. She was, in the words of her father, 'a very good child, always cheerful and full of fun.'

She was brought up on an 800-acre farming estate (now said to have a capital value of £2 million) just outside the village of Dummer, near Basingstoke in the north-east of Hampshire.

But the pleasure Sarah derived from her expansive home stamping-ground was purely domestic, and she became well-known by the three hundred or so inhabitants of the tiny, picturesque village for her bright, bubbling good nature. 'A jolly, sprightly girl who makes me laugh and can take a joke herself,' the

church caretaker said of Sarah, while the chairman of the local parish council praised the way she and her sister were brought up to 'talk to the cowman and ploughman in the same polite way as they would to members of titled families.'

As if aware that she would one day be a member of the Royal Family, she took to horses at the royally early age of three. For stimulus and encouragement in this field she has her mother to thank: Susan Ferguson was not only an excellent and competent horsewoman herself, but also very anxious that her children should share her enthusiasm for this pastime. Sarah let no grass grow under her feet, graduating from Pony Club events to gymkhanas, then junior trials, with determination and speed, eagerly collecting shelvesful of cups, trophies and rosettes along the way. Sometimes she was rather too eager, showing a tendency to tank hell-for-leather towards fences and obstacles, and finishing up horseless, a crashed bundle of frustration furiously walloping the ground with her crop for all she was worth.

A Royal Family

A country girl at heart, Sarah will feel very much at home with her in-laws. Though they show their emotions in public only rarely, they form a close and affectionate family unit within the privacy of their country homes – Windsor Castle, Sandringham, Balmoral, Highgrove and the Castle of Mey. Buckingham Palace has rarely been regarded as 'home' by royalty. It is at Windsor that the Queen prefers to spend her family weekends and which she opens to all her relations at Christmas. Sandringham offers the immediate family a New Year's break during the pheasant-shooting season. Balmoral provides a remote Scottish retreat where the Queen, her children and grandchildren spend long summer weeks. They usually travel there in the Royal Yacht, which almost invariably stops at Scrabster so that everyone can call in on the Queen Mother at her Castle of Mey – one of the happiest family reunions of the year. Andrew and Sarah – seen (these pages) at Windsor in May – will have the use of all these homes, but for real privacy they may choose to stay in any of the outlying lodges and cottages, just as Charles and Diana spend weekends at Sandringham's Wood Farm, or Craigowan Lodge on the Balmoral estate.

Her education was a comparatively mild business. At the age of five she went off to her first school – Daneshill, near Basingstoke – which, then as now, catered for around 200 children, and which Sarah's half-brother, seven-year-old Andrew and half-sister Alice, aged five, now attend. Her headmistress, Miss June Vallance, singled her out as a great sports fiend with courage to spare. She

as light-hearted as it may seem. In 1973, when Sarah was only thirteen, her mother left home to share her life with an Argentinian professional polo player, Hector Barrantes. Predictably, Susan's departure and the divorce proceedings that followed it were traumatic: 'a bit of a fright, to put it mildly, for everyone,' said Ronald later. Neither Sarah nor her sister had suspected what might happen, and it

was left to their father to break the news to them after the event. 'I don't know how I told them that their mother had gone,' he said. 'I just know the feeling, knowing that she'd left me with two girls.' For Jane it was a time of terrible insecurity, and she drew close to Sarah as few older sisters do.

Sarah herself was deeply upset by her mother's disappearance, but did not

The Ring

Sarah's engagement ring consists of a single, large Burmese ruby set amid ten drop diamonds, on a band of white and yellow gold. Made by Garrards, the Queen's jewellers, it is reputed to be worth at least £25,000. Prince Andrew helped to design the ring, and the couple chose the ruby because Sarah has red hair.

proved a reasonably successful all-rounder in class, though with no great academic promise.

By the time she settled in at secondary school – the exclusive, small, red-brick Hurst Lodge at Sunningdale in Berkshire – she had gathered round her a large complement of friends and evolved a mature and sympathetic personality. It was because of this, because of her adult sense of responsibility, her helpfulness and sense of organisation, that in 1976, her final year, she was chosen as head girl.

'We have so many girls coming and going that it is easy to forget them,' said one of her teachers, 'but nobody ever forgot Sarah.' Nor did she leave without qualifications: she picked up six 'O' levels – in Art, English Language, English Literature, Spoken English, French and Biology – and CSEs in Maths and Geography. But she never pursued her academic education further. 'What? 'A' levels?' she once said. 'You must be joking!'

Not all of her school career had been

Even during her visit with Andrew to Northern Ireland (previous pages) Sarah looked as relaxed and happy as (opposite) on her engagement day. (Left) a quiet moment with Andrew.

react openly, and bravely hid her feelings. Her teachers vouch for the fact that they would have known nothing about it had they not been informed officially, and her father found her much more readily adaptable to a home life lacking the pivot of a wife and mother. This may have been primarily because, being a weekly boarder at Hurst Lodge, her day-by-day existence changed very little, but on the other hand, Major Ronald's contribution was probably incalculable. Aware of his daughters' vulnerability, and knowing in his heart of hearts that 'it doesn't matter what the father is like or how much he takes upon himself, or what he does, there is no substitute whatever for a mother at that age', he strove to to his best.

Fortunately, he had the steel to cope with the situation, and he was blest with daughters who were fundamentally easy-going. But he was determined to keep what remained of the family as a unit, and to see that Sarah was not embittered by the experience. That was not easy, with some so-called family friends drifting off and withdrawing their support for fear of being tainted by the whiff of scandal, and with a wife who was content to dispense advice to him without having the responsibility of carrying it out in practice. So there was, as he admitted, 'the odd trying moment, but I hope the girls never realised how tough it was.'

It is a sign of the maturity of the daughter as well as proof that time can heal, that Sarah still feels very close to her mother even though they see each other only rarely. The two get on extremely well together, despite the understandable and irreversible change in their relationship in the last dozen years or so. But, while sister Jane's sense of dependence led to an early marriage – at the age of eighteen she married another polo player, Alex Makim, and the couple went off to farm in Australia – Sarah, being of younger years, had to rely almost solely on her father. Their respect and admiration for each other dates from this time, and Ronald is quietly gratified these days that 'we talk about everything and, of course, she consults me.'

She will probably always be grateful to him for never having attempted to compensate for the domestic upheaval by spoiling her. Never an over-indulgent father, he was aware that to spend his way out of the trials of readjustment would merely have added a mistaken set of values and priorities to the uncertainty that Sarah undoubtedly felt then. For all his protective affection for her he knew that there was no time like the present for teaching her, as he put it, 'to stand on her own two feet'.

(Opposite) Sarah, the latest royal Sloane, may have to give up her liking for the loose, casual, wrap-round look.

'...The Stars in their Courses'

SARAH (Libra)

This marriage brings Sarah radical lifestyle changes just when her mental development will accelerate tremendously. Her Sun in Libra and Moon in Aries show that personal relations are important, that she demands an active part in making decisions and strives to live up to public expectations. Librans being keen on beauty and fashion, her appearance will change sharply with advice from top designers. She and Andrew are both strong-willed with their own ideas on how to live life, but chart comparisons indicate harmonious solutions to problems. They will never be bored together. Children will prove a great joy, and though Sarah is not exactly motherly, she will be actively concerned to ensure their upbringing and education in a protected, peaceful environment.

ANDREW (Pisces)

Andrew was born exactly on the Aquarius/Pisces cusp combining a need for independence and a love of the untried with warm-hearted sympathy. In this marriage of love and mutual romantic attraction, he will not find it easy to accept restrictions and will continue to surprise by unconventional, even rebellious actions. A sensitive, creative person seeking positive ways of self-expression, he will be an attentive, loving husband, protective of Sarah, and concerned for her well-being. His playful, mischievous nature will never cease to amuse and amaze her, and his children (at least two) will be very lucky to have him as a father. He likes to be in charge, but Sarah, who likes to organise and knows her own mind, will find ways of getting what she wants.

He clearly succeeded, for less than three years after his divorce, he felt able to marry again. His second wife was another Susan – former debutante Susan Deptford – and the daughter of a Cambridgeshire farmer. Over fifteen years Ronald's junior (and only twelve years older than Sarah), she proved the ideal stepmother. She ploughed no furrows of her own, accepted the fact that, in any household, two teenage stepdaughters might prove an obstacle to a trouble-free marriage, and adopted a low profile. Placid and understanding by nature, she found it easy to listen to Sarah's adolescent woes and to help her through the problems of growing up. By the time Jane had married and Sarah, having reached her eighteenth birthday, was on the look-out for a job, Ronald and Susan decided to start a family of their own.

In her search for employment, Sarah went straight to Queen's Secretarial College in Kensington where, although she was found to be 'a bit slapdash' at times, she impressed by her ready acceptance of responsibility,

Andrew passes-out at Dartmouth (below) in 1980. In 1982 he returns from the Falklands (below right). Now in 1986, he and Sarah attend a gala in aid of King George's Fund for Sailors.

Senior Service

The Royal Family's Navy links go back to Henry VII, who developed it in the 15th century. Henry VIII strengthened it; Elizabeth I secured England's freedom with it. Charles II and James II were devoted to the sea and ships, while George III's brother and two sons (William IV and Queen Victoria's father) served in the Navy. Victoria's, Edward VII's and George V's second sons all chose naval careers, as did Prince Philip, his Mountbatten uncle and grandfather.

demonstrated that she had initiative, and charmed by a personality which, they said, 'she will well use to her advantage when she gets older.' Subsequent employers were inclined to agree. A Covent Garden art dealer for whom she worked in 1981 confirmed that she did everything with great energy and tremendous speed, while Peter Cunard, the head of a sports public relations agency where she was later employed, found her so keen to get things done that she was always prepared to work late when necessary. What was more, she was never afraid of anybody, and was always 'up front'.

She also worked for a small flat-letting agency in Knightsbridge, but since 1984 has been a member of the firm of BCK, a graphic arts publishing company in Mayfair's George Street – an area much favoured by younger members of the Royal Family in their search for careers. Her responsibilities included assembling catalogues and publicity material, and the company's director, Richard Burton, soon found that she could cope with the job with the minimum of supervision, and that since all she needed was a desk, a telephone and a little direction from the boss, she could in fact work quite easily from home.

Home for Sarah, the working girl, was a chintzy, two-bedroom flat, part of an

its three storeys shielded by unpretentious net curtains. Sarah shared the flat with one of her few firm friends, Carolyn Beckwith-Smith, a cousin of the Princess of Wales' senior Lady-in-Waiting. Coincidentally, Carolyn herself was already engaged to an Old Etonian, Harry Cotterell, who runs a laundry valet service in Chelsea.

Sarah's social life was as busy as her workdays, and hardly suffered from her increasing work-load. In fact, one of her employers was later to recall that she used to spend an inordinate amount of time on the telephone arranging all sorts of evenings and weekends with her friends. It was typical Sloane Ranger behaviour – a stream of social contacts,

Sarah's working wardrobe will undergo a great change to include magnificent evening dresses like the one she wore for a formal portrait in April (right) and the soft, frilled gown seen at Luton Hoo in June (previous page).

Edwardian terraced house in Lavender Gardens, Clapham. A longish, typically turn-of-the-century suburban street, Lavender Gardens is squeezed parallel with a dozen others between the main A3 road into Central London and the film-famous Lavender Hill, equidistant from

Clapham Junction to the north-west and Clapham Common to the south-east.

The house – number 40 – is unexceptional, the dull tint of its outer walls brightened by the occasional artistic flourish of stone carvings and loud red-brick dressings, and the windows of

never-ending ideas for living life to the full, and endless gossip about people, places and fashion. She and her fellow Sloanes searched out the best – or at least, the most fashionable – restaurants and discos, and trailed round the fashion houses and stores of Knightsbridge and

Long before her wedding, Sarah had been seen many times with the Royal Family en masse – an Easter service at Windsor, the Fanfare for Elizabeth gala for the Queen's sixtieth birthday, the State Banquet for the President of Germany at Buckingham Palace. At Royal Ascot, she joined Princess Margaret (top) and Princess Anne (above) in the royal landaus, and mingled with the Queen, the Duke and Duchess of Gloucester and Prince Michael (opposite page) in the Royal Enclosure. (Right) A pre-wedding exit from church for a wide-eyed girl, dressed for her future royal role.

Chelsea for clothes in the very best Diana Spencer tradition.

It was not, however, an irresponsible, spendthrift existence. Sarah's father was at pains to point out that, in line with his policy of not spoiling her, he gave her only a meagre allowance – 'and when I say meagre, I mean meagre' – to top up a modest income from a trust which his own father set up for his granddaughters. Sarah's weekends did not have to be

Sporting Life

Like many members of the Royal Family, Sarah enjoys ski-ing: it was her appearance at Klosters with Charles and Diana that fuelled rumours of her engagement to Andrew. She has also enjoyed the royal pastime of horse-riding since the age of 3, and as a girl took part in Pony Club events, junior trials and gymkhanas. Andrew's sporting horizons are broader: at school he played hockey and rugby and took part in athletics: today he likes sailing and shooting and will occasionally try his luck at cricket. Like Sarah, he is a keen skier – and they both love disco-dancing. And Andrew's artistic flair for photography is matched by Sarah's work in graphic arts.

expensive affairs: she was always welcome back home at Dummer Down Farm, where her stepsister and brother (a third child – Eliza – was born to Ronald and Susan in 1985) found, and still find, her an indulgent, fun companion. Meanwhile, on the social front, she enjoyed enough friendships of the right kind to be invited to house-parties all over Britain in the comfortable country houses of well-to-do and well-connected families.

In June 1985 she was invited to the

most prestigious house-party of all – the Queen's week-long family-and-friends gathering at Windsor Castle during Ascot Week. Guards Polo Club, as it normally does, ran a three-day tournament at Windsor during the same week, and Major Ronald was there as usual watching his protege, Prince Charles, play. So in a sense it was natural that Sarah should, for once, be invited to join the Queen as the daughter of a family friend. Added to which, of course, she was a close friend of the Queen's daughter-in-law – a fact which was later to give rise to the erroneous story that Diana played Cupid from then onwards.

No-one has yet claimed or admitted responsibility for seating Sarah next to Prince Andrew at dinner, but that now famous mock spat over who should eat the profiteroles became what Andrew later described as 'the humble beginning' for a romance. He didn't know it then, or indeed for another six months. In fact, when he was interviewed one afternoon in September for the radio programme *Woman's Hour*, he declared that there was no-one on the horizon as a future wife, but that when he met the girl he wanted to marry, he would know immediately – it would hit him like a lightning bolt.

The question of his marriage was nothing if not timely for, by then, Andrew was well past his twenty-fifth birthday – and hence he was no longer obliged to seek the Queen's consent to marry. Perhaps for that reason, his 25th birthday had been loudly hailed the previous February, the congratulations and speculation being accompanied by long and sometimes nostalgic backward glances over his comparatively short, but certainly eventful life.

Naturally, his birth was heralded, announced and welcomed in circumstances very different from those in which Sarah came into the world. For four days before his arrival, quite large crowds hugged the railings of Buckingham Palace in a loyal attempt to be there when the news was given. One man brought with him a portable record player, complete with a recording of *Land*

of Hope and Glory to play on it when the announcement came.

On a more mundane level, the British public were speculating on whether the new Prince, born at 3.30 on a sleety February afternoon, would be given the title of Duke of York, whether President Eisenhower would be one of his godfathers, or whether the Queen would draw the 18/- (90p) family allowance to which she was now entitled. No, said Buckingham Palace to that one

The names for the new baby had been hotly guessed at since well before the birth. If Andrew was floated at all, it came a long, long way down everybody's list, well after the Alberts, Jameses and Edwards. True to a tradition which has

Queen – justifying the oft-quoted description, 'radiant' – holding a fine, contented infant and surrounded by husband and children looking proud and happy, and it became an immediate classic among royal portfolios.

At the beginning of August, Andrew's grandmother, Queen Elizabeth the Queen Mother, celebrated her sixtieth birthday. The anniversary provoked the sort of rash of eulogies to which we have all become accustomed in each of the years following her 70th birthday, but it lacked the vaguely official character that, for instance, characterised the Queen's own sixtieth birthday in April 1986. And in keeping with the domestic nature of the occasion, the Queen Mother invited her

Sarah and Andrew join the Queen at the Windsor Horse Show just three weeks after her first appearance on the Palace balcony for her 60th birthday. (Over) the Queen and her troops at the 1986 Birthday Parade – the first that Sarah attended.

now happily been discontinued, it was not until over a month after his birth that his names were announced. They were Andrew (after Prince Philip's father, Prince Andrew of Greece), Albert (after the Queen's father, known as Prince Albert until he became Duke of York in 1920), Christian (after King Christian IX of Denmark, the great-great grandfather of both the Queen and Prince Philip), and Edward (after King Edward VII). In those days when relations between the Royal

Family and the exiled Duke of Windsor were a matter of frequent controversy, it did not take long for someone to point out that all of Prince Andrew's names were also borne by the former King Edward VIII, and to wonder whether this was not tempting fate!

With the announcement of the names came an album of 'official' photographs, taken by Cecil Beaton a few days earlier in the Music room of Buckingham Palace. It was a delightful selection, showing the

grandchildren Charles and Anne to Clarence House to have their pictures taken with her. At the last moment, the Queen thought it would be nice to send the baby along too, and so young Andrew found himself wriggling on the Queen Mother's knee as the photographer snapped away. Gummy smiles, curling toes, blond fluffy hair – this was the stuff to put into a nation's newspapers next morning.

Barring another set of family

photographs taken the following month, with Andrew joining the Queen, Prince Philip and their elder children on a tartan plaid rug spread out on the lawn of Balmoral Castle, public sightings of Andrew were few and far between. Opportunities were limited to family holidays, when train journeys to or from Scotland and Sandringham offered a glimpse of the Prince and excuse for speculating on his progress. Though this low-key exposure was well-meant, it tended to backfire at times when, for want of positive proof of his good health, the lack of first-hand information was taken as an indication that there might just be (in the tactful phraseology of the time) 'something wrong' with the Queen's third child.

Eventually, people came to terms with the prospect of seeing very little of their young prince. With busy parents, and siblings ten or more years older than he,

his life at Buckingham Palace was hardly enviable, for all the comfort and material security it offered, but he was soon able to enjoy the company of a virtual platoon of cousins, as first Princess Margaret, then Princess Alexandra, then the Duchess of Kent, married and had children. And in 1964 – the Year of the Royal Babies – his mother presented him with a baby brother. From then on, with the veneer of responsibility for young Prince Edward, Andrew seems to have become a more self-assured youngster.

As his elder brother and sister temporarily disappeared from the scene into their private schools, Andrew seemed to emerge into public consciousness. Whether tricked out in emerald green velvet as page-boy at the Marquess of Hamilton's wedding at the age of six, or watching work on the new Hovercraft on the Isle of Wight two years later, he was at last seen with satisfying

A bright hour on a damp day: Andrew and Sarah, newly engaged, in the garden of Buckingham Palace.

frequency and, more important, in an acceptable light.

The year 1968 seems to have been something of a turning point. In it, he joined the First Marylebone Cub Scout pack, emulating the sense of service in early age which had led Princess Anne into the Brownies. He was taken to several public and ceremonial events at Windsor, and royal sporting outings – polo, Braemar, the Windsor Horse Show – soon seemed incomplete without him. In September the Queen and Duke of Edinburgh took him to his first school, Heatherdown, near Ascot, where he was met in the full glare of media publicity by the headmaster in the school grounds. Oddly, the snapping of cameras failed to

Sarah's nearly-royal status secured her a seat in the royal box at Wimbledon in July. On this occasion (top) she invited along Carolyn Beckwith-Smith, her former Clapham flatmate. As it happened, Carolyn had just beaten Sarah in the engagement stakes, and it was to her wedding (above and left) to Harry Cotterell at Holy Trinity Church, Rudgwick in Sussex that Sarah took Andrew (top left) on 5th July.

unnerve him: suited in regulation charcoal grey with light blue shirt and scarlet tie and cap, Andrew fairly oozed confidence, seeming to take the whole occasion so much in his stride that it augured well for his immediate future.

Naturally, life was very different from his previous educational existence. Here was no governess to teach him basic subjects in an exclusive class of four or five relatives and friends, but a rota of masters detailed to treat him like hundreds of other boys, drive knowledge of a dozen or more subjects into him, and coach him in five or six sporting disciplines. Instead of retiring at night to his own small suite of Palace rooms, he shared a dormitory with six other boys, and endured the occasional ribbing and somewhat less cosy routine that goes with public school life.

For all that, life was not so bad and there were the occasional moments of high excitement. Irish terrorism in the early 1970s led to Andrew's being protected day and night by Special Branch police officers (as was his cousin George, Earl of St Andrew's, who joined the school two years after he did). There was the famous incident of the school outing punch-up, when a group of Heatherdown boys in Andrew's school party were involved in a fight with other boys during a visit to the Natural History Museum in London. And there was the time in 1971 when Andrew became the school's first television star, after he had appeared with the Queen and Prince Edward, thumbing through the royal family album during the royal Christmas message.

Academically, Andrew proved no brighter that his elder brother, though his sporting abilities matched his tremendous enthusiasm for competitive games. Already a sound swimmer and keen sailor – by now he was a regular visitor to Cowes Week with his father – he ultimately represented his school in the senior rugby and cricket teams. It seemed to provide him with good enough credentials for Gordonstoun, and that was where he went in the Autumn of 1973.

Outgoing, extrovert, active and competitive, Andrew fitted the school's sensible new regime handsomely.

The Fergusons

The Fergusons are of Gaelic origin so, like Diana, Sarah brings Irish blood into the Royal Family. Like her, too, Sarah can claim royal blood, as both descend from Charles II: one of his mistresses is Diana's forebear; another, Lucy Walters, is Sarah's. Through her father's father Sarah is the Duke of Gloucester's cousin; another ancestor wed into the Lascelles family into which the Queen's aunt, the Princess Royal, married; and Sarah is also the Queen Mother's fifth cousin three times removed. She is also related to Sam Whitbread, the brewery founder, to Bess of Hardwick, a ruthless political opportunist of Tudor times, and to Mrs Fitzherbert, yet another royal mistress – George IV's. No doubt ancestral Ferguson ghosts rejoice that Sarah's liaison is royal *and* respectable!

Socially, he still had a lot to learn, the tendency towards arrogance which Heatherdown teachers had observed with concern some years earlier becoming as much a handicap as being trailed from pillar to post by his personal detectives or being fawned upon or snubbed by colleagues, depending upon what view they took of his royal status. And as time went on, he found that rarely could he form even the most innocent and platonic of attachments to members of the opposite sex – the thirty girls in the school in 1973 increased in number annually – without grossly inaccurate or exaggerated stories reaching the press.

Indeed it was at about this time that his fast-developing good looks and easy

manner with the girls began to earn him the reputation of a royal ladies' man. For several months there was serious speculation that he was already destined to marry Amanda Knatchbull, a granddaughter of Lord Mountbatten, who had joined the school at the same time as Andrew. It was not, considering Mountbatten's almost lifelong ambition to keep his family linked with the Windsors, a bad long shot but, like many subsequent tales of what was supposed to have gone on behind Gordonstoun's well-guarded doors, it proved well wide of the mark.

In a move similar to that taken with regard to Prince Charles, Andrew spent a couple of terms in 1977 abroad, in one of Gordonstoun's exchange arrangements. Whereas the elder brother had gone to Australia, the younger was sent to Canada for a six-month spell at Lakefield College in Ontario. The college's 'healthy mind, healthy body' motto found expression in vigorous physical opportunities, from cross-country ski-ing to kayaking, and in constant encouragement towards intellectual pursuits.

Always a doer rather than a spectator, and eager to try anything once, Andrew took to the college's ways like a duck to water. He joined its hockey team (and was 'suitably vicious when necessary'), continued with a pottery course he had started at Gordonstoun, proved himself 'really first class' on skis, joined a windsurfing group, and did some white water paddling on the Petawa river.

But here, as at Gordonstoun, it wasn't long before his interest in the country's female population – or possibly more correctly, their interest in him – took over. He had already, much to his embarrassment, found himself the focus of an hysterical reception from teenage girls on his very arrival in Toronto, but that was only the beginning. When he went skiing with a Lakefield pupil, Martha Anderson, she was in the eyes of the press as good as engaged to him. Andrew countered by arranging a reunion with Sandi Jones, who had been his companion during his previous year's visit to Montreal for the 1976 Olympics. He took her sailing, then to a reception, then to a jazz concert in Toronto, and finally to

a college dance, where he infuriated all the other girls there by dancing almost exclusively with her. Oblivious of their pique, he gave Sandi his college scarf and a badge to remember him by.

The recounting of such incidents added fuel to the fires of popular passions. Hordes of young, moon-struck girls hopped along the boundaries of cricket and rugby pitches, screaming for the sporting prince in his natty flannels or trim shorts, and half-swooned every time he flashed what one described as 'his toothy smile' at them. And when on one occasion he went to Pittsburgh to support his college hockey team, the attentions lavished on him by the local girls made him the arch-enemy, for the day at least, of their boyfriends.

Despite the occasional sour note – 'I do hope he brought his woollies,' jeered a newspaper columnist after Andrew had intended a joke about Canada's weather – he throughly enjoyed Canada. He found time to travel westwards and northwards, visiting the Pacific coast and the Arctic. He saw how the Eskimos build kayaks and prepare polar bear skins for tanning, visited three major wildlife parks, was proclaimed 'Heir of the Earth' by the Algonquin Indians, and hooked – then lost – his first salmon off Victoria. That the total experience was one he relished both at the time and as a memory, is proved by the fact that it brought him voluntarily back to Canada six years later.

In mid-1983, his former headmaster at Lakefield organised a great-outdoors expedition along the Nahanni River in the Northwest Territories' Mackenzie Mountains, and invited Andrew to join some twenty college students, former students and members of staff. He seized the opportunity with both hands, and for the best part of three weeks he canoed his way along fast-flowing rivers, shooting rapids, negotiating dangerous waterfalls, and paddling through canyons hundreds of metres deep for over two hundred miles. Added to that were miles of back-packing through wilderness and wild bear country, and in weather that was less than kind. One spell of torrential rain lasted for no less than three days, but it only drew out Andrew's sense of humour: dripping wet in green combat trousers, an old shirt, black Army boots and a

Different life styles: (left) Andrew with Senior Service shipmates; (above) Sarah leaving home for work. New life style: it's palaces and panoply (opposite) for Sarah from now on.

shapeless, bottle-green camouflage hat, he said: 'I shall have to speak to mother about fixing this weather!'

'Not being first in line to the Throne,' wrote Rosalie Shann of the *Sunday Graphic* two days after Andrew was born, 'the Prince will obviously be able to choose his own career. And I wouldn't be in the least surprised if, within fifteen years from this date, we had another sailor Prince in the Royal Family. Imagine how delighted Prince Philip would be!' It was, of course, a pretty safe guess, even if the timing was four years out. But, true to form, the second son of the sovereign took to the Royal Navy once again. Early

in 1979, Andrew applied to join the Senior Service and was accepted in May of that year for a twelve-year short service commission as a helicopter pilot. In September he entered the Royal Naval

(Previous pages) Andrew and Sarah pictured at Buckingham Palace. (These pages) a day of celebration second only to his wedding: Andrew's Falklands return is greeted by the Queen.

Training College at Dartmouth for a four-month course, and comfortably passed his qualifying exams. He 'passed out' of Dartmouth in April 1980, and the Queen came to take the Salute at the passing-out parade and inspect the guard of honour of which he formed part. Needless to say, neither mother nor son could resist a brief smile as the Queen walked past.

It seems at first sight a contradiction that, having joined the Navy, Andrew should spend most of his career flying helicopters. It marks not only the way the Navy has changed since the days when it was associated wholly and solely with ships, but also Andrew's versatility and open-mindedness. While in his final years at Gordonstoun (which he left in 1979 with 'A' level passes in English, History and

Economics & Political Science), he had learned to fly gliders, had been awarded his parachutist's badge after a Royal Air Force course, and had been taught to fly to solo standard in a two-week course at RAF Benson. Now, his naval career pushed him further towards his goal of combining flight and sailing – of, as he once put it, 'living to fly, and to fly from the sea.'

Within a year of his passing out from Dartmouth, not only had he successfully completed a four-month flying training course in a Bulldog aircraft and his basic helicopter flying training at Culdrose in Cornwall, but he also took the prize for the best pilot on the course. Prince Philip was there to present him with his wings, and looked as delighted as the *Sunday Graphic's* prophet had foretold two decades earlier. It was then that his definitive career as a qualified and trained helicopter pilot began, though at the time he had little inkling of what 1982 was to bring.

In April of that year he was suddenly called off Easter leave, which he was spending at Windsor Castle, to join the general alert after the Argentinians had invaded the Falkland Islands. The prospect of his actually going to war prompted hasty consultations between the Ministry of Defence, the Prime Minister and the Queen, as to whether it was wise to send Andrew into possible battle, but the Queen was in no mood to prevaricate on this supreme question of duty. Nor was Andrew's commanding officer, who barked uncompromisingly, 'Prince Andrew is a serving officer and will do whatever is required of him. He's a member of my crew and flies like any other man. That's the way we play it.'

The Argentinians, already cock-a-hoop at having stolen a march on the British, derided Andrew's approach as his ship, HMS *Invincible* joined the Task Force from Portsmouth, announcing the imminent arrival of 'the Crown Prince of Colonialism' who 'should have brought

*After his safe homecoming from the Falklands, Andrew's first Cenotaph wreath bore a label in remembrance of British servicemen killed there.
(Opposite) Sarah chose a sailor-style dress for an official engagement photograph.*

Task Force Log

Prince Andrew was called up from leave on 3rd April, 1982 and next day sailed with almost 1,000 colleagues on board the 19,500-ton aircraft carrier HMS *Invincible* from Portsmouth. *Invincible* arrived off the Falklands late that month. As a member of 820 Helicopter Squadron, Andrew's duties involved reconnaissance flying, seeking and rescuing survivors of naval encounters, and acting as decoy for enemy missiles. The Falklands were recaptured on 14th June, but *Invincible* and her crew stayed on until August, returning to Portsmouth on 17th September after 166 days' away. For his part in the conflict, Andrew was awarded the South Atlantic Medal, and has associated himself with the Falklands Appeal and the South Atlantic Fund in their attempts to alleviate physical and financial suffering among thousands of wounded soldiers and the dependent families of the 256 who died.

his nappies with him.' Meanwhile 'H', as Andrew was called, prepared for an onslaught that was not long in coming. At the end of April he was out rescuing a crewman from his sister ship *Hermes*, whose helicopter was lost, and was flying over the wreck of HMS *Sheffield*, the first major casualty of the conflict. The sight of wreckage and carnage, and smell of smoke and fumes are engraved on his memory to this day, and he swears he will never forget it.

From that point he was out on a round-the-clock duty involving reconnaissance, rescue, and acting as a decoy for the Exocet missiles of the sort that had destroyed *Sheffield*. Experiencing war at first hand, and being as vulnerable as anyone in the conflict that killed over 250 Britons, made him feel indefinably 'different'. 'I think my life has gone round the corner since I left for the Falklands. I felt lonely more than anything else. When you are down on the deck, when there are missiles flying around, then at that precise moment you are on your own and that's all there is. On the odd occasion I was terrified. To overcome fear I tried to adopt a positive mental attitude. I can't actually remember what I thought of – what I put in my mind – but I just remember telling myself, "I am going to survive this."'

Survive he did, as did *Invincible's* crew of almost a thousand souls. And when they came back to Britain after almost six months' absence, the Queen was there to greet them – and him. So were thousands of their relatives, encapsulating their collective relief and patriotism in banners like the one addressed to the Queen which announced: 'Well done, Mum; we're glad Andy's home.'

'Home' was a relative term. Andrew has, since then, and for one reason or another, been away from Britain almost as often as not. Naval duties have taken him to the Americas and the West Indies, holidays to the Caribbean and Canada, official duties to St Helena, Ascension Island, the United States and Canada again. He has hardly been in any one place long enough for anyone to speculate seriously about his getting spliced. Which is why, when he was spotted escorting Sarah Ferguson into

the Royal Enclosure at Ascot on that sunny June day in 1985, there was just a ripple of rumour – nothing more – that here might be the Queen's next daughter-in-law.

It was not until the turn of the year that the ripple became a wave. Sarah was invited to spend part of the Royal Family's New Year break with them at Sandringham. The press were stiffened into a sense of duty which never fails them at times like these, and they surrounded the private estate as if their lives depended on it. They were duly rewarded when, through long lenses, they distinguished Andrew and Sarah walking together so close that they could well have been holding hands – and that, for royalty, was enough to set the pulses racing.

The Diana syndrome took over from there. Sarah's Clapham home and the Mayfair office where she worked, the George Street sandwich bar where she used to have lunch, and the discos she frequented became obligatory waiting points for photographers and journalists alike. Predictably, there were no further clues in the hide-and-seek game until the truly unexpected occurred – and by royal instigation. In early February, Prince Charles and his family went to see Andrew on board his latest ship, HMS *Brazen*, then on a courtesy visit to the Pool of London. It was a private engagement as royal engagements go, but the rarity of seeing the whole Wales family out in public brought the press out in force. The unexpected bonus – Sarah in tow, even though ostensibly as Diana's companion – bestowed upon the press all the confirmation it could have asked for.

When the Prince and Princess of Wales

Sarah's fiery locks have made red hair almost nationally fashionable. And she proves that you don't necessarily have to spend hours at the hairdresser to show it all off to the best advantage!

went to Klosters for a skiing holiday almost directly afterwards, and lined up for their customary photo-call with Sarah once again only metres away, there was the feeling that she was either the future Princess Andrew or the most shameless red herring Buckingham Palace had ever thrown the media's way. She was swamped by flashing cameras and shouted questions when she returned to London a few days later, and from then was given a police escort to and from work (which prompted one churl to ask whether this was because her life was in danger – or were the Metropolitan Police now providing a chaperone service?)

Days of high-season sun, fun, colour and fashion. Sarah turned heads with her own selection of headgear and a very individual dress as she joined the Queen (top), the Queen Mother (above right) and Princess Michael (right) at Ascot in June.

They need not have worried on either count. No-one loves a lover more than the press, and Sarah seemed almost to be revelling in the publicity. Like Diana before her, she fielded all the usual questions with polite good humour and infuriating discretion. Once her car failed to start; another time she had difficulty getting out of a tight parking space; on other occasions she had to drive almost recklessly fast to lose her pursuers. Yet, without exception, she handled them all with tight-lipped, unprotesting confidence and aplomb.

'It has been quite an ordeal for a country girl,' said her father, when it was all over. 'I am extremely proud of her. She has behaved absolutely perfectly, never holding her head down, always being

'Everyone loves a story like this...' – and sent a telegram to the happy couple to say that the engagement 'would give great joy throughout the country.' Sarah's grandmother, Lady Elmhirst, said that the family was 'very happy indeed and very honoured. It's a nice fairy tale.'

Andrew's shipmates on *Brazen* received the news direct from the groom-to-be by telephone. By all accounts he sounded as bubbly as the champagne they broke open to celebrate, though it might have been otherwise had he realised that he had not closed his mess bill and his colleagues were counting on putting the cost of the celebration on it. Pupils at Daneshill School were allowed to watch the couple being interviewed on television. Staff at

advertisement appeared on behalf of the makers of Ferguson televisions. 'Trust a Ferguson to get a good reception at the Palace!' it trumpeted, adding proudly that their sets now came 'with something no other set can match – the bride's name on the front.'

Somehow, this seemed to say it all. Sarah was already a household name and would soon follow Diana into that world of transition from relatively unknown

Last pre-wedding balcony appearance: Andrew and Sarah line up with Princess Margaret, the Queen Mother, Prince and Princess Michael, the Queen, Prince Philip, Princess Alice, the Grand Duke and Duchess of Luxemburg and Charles and Diana after the Trooping in June.

polite, always smiling, yet never giving anything away.' His reaction, though he confessed himself 'reasonably emotional', was about the quietest of anybody's that day. Prince Charles said he could not be more delighted: 'I think she's wonderful... but then, I'm biased.' The Prime Minister oozed her delight –

Dummer's Queen public house concocted a lethal looking cocktail of champagne, orange juice and Monterez liqueur, called it Fergie's Fizz, sold it at £1.20 a glass – purple umbrellas and all – and it flowed like the Thames at high tide.

Meanwhile, the admen were ready and waiting. The following day a full-page

commoner to the wife of a prince of the blood royal. That means facing more than your fair share of publicity, good and bad, toeing a line you may not have realised existed before, and above all having to do as Andrew advised her as she first approached the cameras on that famous visit to HMS *Brazen* – 'Keep smiling!'

Sarah found absolutely no difficulty following Andrew's advice. It was smiles all the way from that drizzly, damp day on which her engagement was announced to the joyful and colourful day on which they were at last married. Part of the reason for those continuing good vibes was that, unlike Diana, Sarah was hardly ever the victim of the press intrusion, unhealthy speculation and curiosity for scandal that her new-sister-in-law, Princess Diana, had suffered so incessantly in 1981. And part was undoubtedly due to the fact that Sarah enjoyed the full and unquestioned support of her fiancé's family. And no-one expressed this support more clearly than Prince Philip, who said he was delighted that Andrew was getting

anyone should complain about that.'

Certainly the British tourist and souvenir industries were in no mood to complain about their immediate prospects when, just six days after the royal engagement, July 23rd was chosen as the date of the wedding. The London Tourist Board was as beside itself as such an august body is ever likely to be, declaring the event and the run-up to it as not only direct attractions for foreign holidaymakers, but worth millions as a long-term publicity booster. It was, as major royal occasions are, a rare opportunity for enterprise. One London coach operator forsook the usual tourist traps and took its customers on a tour of Fergie's London – past the office where she worked, the snack-bar where she

By the dawn of the wedding day several thousands of people had staked out their territories on the pavement of the Mall, Whitehall and Broad Sanctuary. One Staffordshire man had actually spent three nights camping out to claim his spot. Early morning hours were spent being shamelessly patriotic, with loyalists wrapping themselves in the flag (opposite, bottom left). Eventually, Prince Andrew emerged from Buckingham Palace with Prince Edward (right and below). It was smiles all the way to the Abbey (opposite, bottom right) and the Wedding of the Year had begun.

married because 'they seem very happy together, are well adjusted, and I think Sarah will be a great asset. She is fortunate to have established an occupation before joining the family and she's capable of becoming self-employed. I hope Sarah will be able to continue as a sort of consultant, and I don't see why

lunched, the basement winerie where she popped in for a quick drink after work, the restaurants where she dined, Garrard's the royal jewellers where even then her wedding ring was being fashioned from gold mined near Dolgellau in Wales, the solarium and hairdressing salon in Albemarle Street

which she patronised, and that famous terraced house in Clapham which she had by now been obliged to abandon for the security of Buckingham Palace.

The souvenir trade anticipated a field day, their first for five years. The prestigious house of Wedgwood led a potential £200 million market with a

A momentary change in the weather as the royal carriages arrive at Sanctuary Green. Though it stayed favourable, the occasional black cloud kept crowds alert for the odd shower. Meanwhile an airship bearing a "Good Luck" message hovered above Parliament (left).

One of the most spectacular displays of loyalty from the crowds greeted Prince Andrew and Sarah Ferguson at Trafalgar Square (above) where the decorative plinths for Landseer's lions formed a picturesque backdrop. Andrew and his supporter — brother Prince Edward looked pleased (right) and not a little surprised by the affection that they met every inch of the way.

comprehensive range of Staffordshire pottery to suit all pockets – from a £5 sweet dish to an ornate urn costing a hundred times as much – while at the other end of the scale a Sunday newspaper offered a pair of Andrew & Sarah drinking mugs to each of fifty readers who sent in the most entertaining stories about what went disastrously wrong at their own weddings. Commemorative medallions, struck in

everything from cupro-nickel to 22-carat solid gold, flooded the catalogues of medal specialists and coin-dealers world wide, while Cash's designed some impressive woven bookmarks available for no more than £3.50. From Perrett's you could order your very own bunting from a new, specially drawn-up list including fancy street banners and tasselled balcony aprons which proclaimed your loyalty and congratulations to the happy couple, while Liberty's settled for pure silk ties tricked out with naval symbols and English roses as apt substitutes for royal portraits.

Inevitably, some of the more entrepreneurial opportunists went mischievously over the top. A company called Emotional Rescue devised a spoof wedding invitation card calling on guests to repair, after the Abbey service, to the reception at the Pig & Whistle, Shepherds Bush. (Dress: tweeds and green wellies). A

Dorset perfumier created a blend of jasmine, rose and lavender, called it 'Fergie', hailed it as 'A Fragrance of Today' and billed it as designed 'for the fashion-conscious, sophisticated girl about town... fresh, young and vibrant.' Customer reaction, never very enthusiastic, varied from 'rather fun' to 'not all that unusual'. Two girls who claimed to have known Sarah in the past designed a sun hat showing her and Andrew enveloped in a heart-shape, and marketed it through Harrods for £1.99, while the London Diamond Centre offered a replica of Sarah's engagement ring for a mere £5,000.

But for sheer controversy, you could not beat the little matter of the prohibited T-shirt, the one souvenir garment which fell foul of the Queen's personal decision that 'some articles of clothing are not suitable places for royal photographs.' In the absence of any

threat of legal sanctions, one Essex manufacturer went ahead and put Andrew and Sarah on the front of his T-shirts – half a million of them – and adamantly insisted, 'I don't care if they send me to the Tower. I'm a true blue monarchist and this is a chance to bang the drum for England.'

In the meantime, Sarah was beginning her brief, somewhat crowded, but fascinating apprenticeship for a lifelong public demand for her time, patience, patronage, sense of duty, and sympathetic behaviour. For two months, it was as if March 19th had never happened, so rarely was she seen at all. One eagle-eyed photographer snapped her horse-riding with the Queen in Windsor Great Park at the end of March, and she joined the Royal Family for Easter

Stages in Sarah's happy progress from Clarence House to Westminster Abbey. Showing her headdress of heavily perfumed flowers and just a hint of her voluminous dress and train, she rode with her father in the Glass Coach. (Following pages) the bride in Whitehall and Parliament Square, while the Queen and Prince Philip arrive at the Abbey.

service at St George's Chapel Windsor. On 21st April, she was back at St George's to attend the thanksgiving service for the Queen's sixtieth birthday, following which she found herself for the very first time out on the balcony of Buckingham Palace, waving somewhat uncertainly to thousands of schoolchildren as they sang birthday songs to their sovereign. She was much more at home in the palace forecourt later on, when she helped the Queen gather in an endless supply of the children's daffodils, thrilled to be virtually swamped by so much goodwill and youthful, natural curiosity.

But it was not until mid-May that Sarah emerged from her long weeks of making preparations for her wedding and being schooled in the elementary principles of royal life. By then, Andrew had returned from a brief holiday in the Bahamas (he had dashed off the homeward plane in such a hurry to see Sarah again that he left his hand luggage behind), and they were at last able to go about the country together. Dressed unfashionably, but sensibly for that cold, drab month, in warm, thick jackets and Wellingtons, they attended the Royal Windsor Horse Show, then proceeded to Cambridgeshire where Andrew opened the Imperial War Museum's new hangar at Duxford (and where Sarah displayed true delight at receiving the first of a lifetime's supply of bouquets), then to a charity theatre production in Weymouth, a surprise two-day visit to Northern Ireland (an occasional obligation for all members of the Royal Family), to a State Banquet given for the West German President in June, and so on.

But Andrew was still only part way through his eight-week officer training course at Greenwich, so Sarah found herself doing rather more solo turns than Princess Diana had before her wedding in 1981. She went without Andrew to the Chelsea Flower Show in May, and looked rather more absorbed by the exhibits than most of her in-laws normally do. She went to Queen's Club and Wimbledon, taking advantage of the unwritten rule that as a royal (or nearly so!) you have no trouble getting a grandstand seat for the season's best tennis), and she certainly held her fashion head high when, with or without Andrew, she put in some

Among over 1,700 guests were politicians, foreign royalty, Commonwealth diplomats and a host of personal friends including Michael Caine, Antony Andrews and Elton John. Nancy Reagan (left, above and opposite, top left) arrived from the States amid heavy security. Others (right) could afford to linger outside the Abbey – except, that is, for the bridesmaids and pages (opposite, top right). Overleaf: the Prince and Princess of Wales were among the last to arrive, while Sarah, spot on time and not insisting on the bride's prerogative of lateness, found time for a last-minute adjustment which her father and Lindka Cierach, her dressmaker, were eager to attend to.

frequent attendances at a sun-blessed and colourful Royal Ascot.

She allowed herself just one break – a brief holiday in Antigua, where she stayed with her old school-chum Florence Belmondo, whose actor-father Jean-Paul owns a villa there. For just over a week she bathed in the villa's private pool, played tennis on its floodlit courts in the cool of the evenings, gave her sensitive, freckled skin the gentlest of tans on the beach and, accompanied only by a single detective, whizzed round the island's bays at 70 miles an hour in a borrowed speedboat. It was a superb finale to her bachelor-girl days, and she came back to London in early June looking at peak fitness. And when, in her first public appearance thereafter, she stood in for her future mother-in-law and presented the Queen's Cup to Prince Charles' victorious polo team at Smith's

Lawn, she was a picture of health, happiness, laughter, fun and self-assurance.

Which was probably just as well, since it may have been with some trepidation that she realised her wedding was only six weeks away. If so, she need never have worried, for in her absence something close to an army of organisers had been beavering away arranging, for the forthcoming national occasion, what most of us would find pretty daunting at a purely domestic level. The Lord Chamberlain, the Earl of Airlie, had right from the start been busy coordinating everything from the availability of royal carriages to the simple but effective decorations in the Mall which reminded the royal couple, if they ever needed to be reminded, that this was very much *their* day.

Since the decision to hold the

A huge cheer went up as Sarah stepped out of the tiny Glass Coach (above) and made her way into the Abbey to join her straw-hatted pages and prettily-frocked bridesmaids (right). She was undaunted by the vast array of clergy and dignitaries facing her ,and made her steady four-minute progress (overleaf) up the aisle towards the Quire to the tune of Elgar's Imperial March. *She performed her vows almost word perfect (following page, bottom) and looked even more self assured as she returned from signing the Registers, clutching the arm of her husband, to face the Royal Family for the first time as one of their number, and as the latest in a long if somewhat intermittent line of Duchesses of York.*

Like all royal brides before her, Sarah's last duty before she walked from the Sacrarium was to curtsey to the Queen, a manoeuvre achieved (top left) with supreme aplomb and a broad smile! Prince William led the pages and bridesmaids out after her (above), while the camera caught a rare Fergie grimace as she tried to lift her billowing dress and train back into the carriage (right).

wedding in Westminster Abbey (the fourteenth such wedding there since Henry I married Mathilda of Scotland in 1100) limited the guest list to just over 1,700, he had to see that the issue of invitation cards pleased as many, and offended as few, as possible. He had to time every move of the day, from the exit of Guards from their barracks early in the morning to the safe arrival of bride and groom at the Royal Hospital Chelsea late that afternoon, a procedure so minutely detailed that it included allowing just over four minutes each way for the bridal processions in the Abbey, and ten minutes (no more, no less) for the signing of the three registers – royal, ecclesiastical and civil – and all the kisses,

tears and handshakes that such interludes normally involve. He it was, too, who arranged for the three people from St John's Ambulance and a couple of doctors to be placed strategically in the Abbey in case of emergencies.

As it happened, the date he had announced for the wedding didn't suit everybody. The Queen herself had to shuffle one of her prior engagements that day – tea with the Royal Medical Benevolent Fund at St James's Palace – over to the following day's schedule. The Duke of Kent's younger son, Lord Nicholas Windsor, had to plead a previously arranged holiday. The Earl and Countess of Harewood, well established back in the royal fold, had already

committed themselves to a visit to Australia to organise the Adelaide Festival. The Dean and Chapter of Westminster had to transfer an arranged consecration of bishops on the 22nd July to Southwark Cathedral so as not to interfere with the programme for the final wedding rehearsal, whilst regular Abbey services scheduled for the 23rd were moved to neighbouring St Margaret's. Andrew's shipmates on HMS *Brazen* felt somewhat piqued at missing out on the celebrations owing to being on duty in the Middle East. And even the most flamboyant and sunny of Britain's TV astrologers reckoned it would be 'a very mediocre day for both of them. The Queen will not be feeling at her best

either.' Nothing personal, but it was good for all of us that he was proved wrong.

Certainly Sarah and Andrew entertained no such doubts, and if you were at all surprised by the magnificent proliferation of flowers in the Abbey, it is to Sarah that you should direct the credit. When Mrs Pam McNicol, chairman of the National Association of Flower Arrangement Societies, was asked to mastermind the floral decorations, she was quickly relieved of the burden of choosing the flowers. On one of her early walks with Sarah round the Abbey, she found the main decision made for her. 'Lots of roses,' said Sarah (almost as if she knew she was going to be made Duchess of York), 'and more flowers than at any other royal wedding.' Mrs McNicol was delighted, secure in the knowledge that, of all flowers, roses would be available in abundance and at their best at just that time. Andrew pitched in with a few suggestions of his own, including one brainwave – sadly short-lived – in which he envisaged great chains of flowers suspended from the Abbey rafters. Ten out of ten for originality, was the verdict, but thoroughly impracticable. 'I'm afraid we had to water down some of his ideas,' added the Association's president, with genuine regret.

On a more fundamental note, the Archbishop of Canterbury was appointed to marry the couple, and he emphasised their future responsibilities, including the bringing up of their children in the faith, with due solemnity at a private meeting at Lambeth Palace in mid-April. One newspaper columnist thought this advice to be intrusive, that what the newlyweds now do within the privacy of their own marriage should be no concern of the Archbishop's, and that it was 'insulting beyond measure' to imply that they took their vows that day without meaning to keep them. Most people, however, were less grudging, and assumed it was the least the Archbishop could do in order to discharge his own ecclesiastical duty.

Britain's new Duchess of York certainly knew how to respond to the tumultuous reception that awaited her and her husband as they left the Abbey (top) and were driven through the streets of London. Having removed her headdress, thrown back her sequinned silk veil and revealed her tiara (borrowed from a family friend) she revelled in the rejoicing and left the crowd in no doubt of her appreciation.

It was a sunny and light-hearted drive back to Buckingham Palace and both Sarah and Andrew enjoyed the heady atmosphere to the full. At the end of their first journey together as man and wife, Sarah's first act was to give each of her bridesmaids and pages a huge kiss — and they couldn't line up fast enough to be on the receiving end.

By the early part of July, the royal couple had decided to adopt the form of marriage service set out in the 1662 Book of Common Prayer, in which the bride utters what is these days quite a controversial promise to obey her husband, rather than the more modern adaptation omitting that vow, which was used at the marriage of the Prince and Princess of Wales. That earlier marriage was, however, taken as a precedent for the inclusion in the service procedure of the Roman Catholic Archbishop of Westminster, the Moderator of the Church of Scotland, the Chaplain of the Fleet, and representatives of the Free Church Council to make Andrew and Sarah's wedding ceremony as

comprehensively ecumenical as Charles and Diana's.

For the Abbey staff, the fact that, after the disappointment of not hosting the 1981 wedding, they were to be at the centre of these royal nuptials, was cause enough for celebration. At the top the new Dean, Michael Mayne, installed only sixteen days beforehand, was thrilled with this most august of duties so soon after taking up office. For the two hundred people in his charge, from the Chapter to the beadles, here was an

(Above) The Queen Mother, ever popular at almost 86, travels with her younger daughter, Princess Margaret and her children, Lady Sarah Armstrong-Jones and Viscount Linley. For the Prince and Princess of Wales (above right) a carriage to themselves — just like Andrew and Sarah who (opposite page) clearly relieved to be married at last, had time for a quick word with each other as their bridal procession moved into Whitehall.

Triumphal processions follow the bride and groom (above left) back to the Palace. The elder bridesmaids and pages (left) are followed by Prince Philip with Mrs. Susan Barrantes (top & right) mother of the bride, and by the Queen Mother with Princess Margaret and her children.

unforgettable chance to participate in the nation's history. The bellringers were busy practising their three and a half hours of peals on ten bells. The electrical experts began work early in July, helping contractors to lay miles of cable to serve an enormous television coverage which required fairly fierce, but reasonably unobtrusive lighting in the triforium.

Maintenance men had to build rostra for television cameras and additional stands, tucked neatly out of full view, for pressmen and photographers. Two days before the wedding, in came the masses of flowers from growers nationwide, Covent Garden suppliers, the Royal parks and Windsor Castle. And on the final pre-wedding day there was a full-scale rehearsal, complete with almost a hundred ushers – most of them friends of the family, but also including some forty honorary Abbey stewards, for whom one day such as this is worth years of volunteering.

By then, the splendid blue carpet, last used for the Order of the Bath Service two months earlier, was back in place, the blue and white striped awning (which

Opposite page: the view from the top of Admiralty Arch as the Duke and Duchess of York's 1902 State Landau bowls round from Whitehall into the Mall. Left: Major Ronald Ferguson showing no sign of the emotional state he confidently expected to experience, as he drives back to Buckingham Palace with the Queen. Above: Postillions keep a straight face and a wary eye as Princess Anne and Captain Mark Phillips wave to the crowd on their return journey.

Andrew and Sarah had agreed in May should be sideless, so as to allow everyone as full a view of the emerging bridal couple as possible) was erected, and the staff of the Clerk of Works had rehearsed for the last time the raising of the Royal Standard, ready for the precise moment when the Queen, on her way to her son's wedding, crossed the invisible threshold from public property in Victoria Street onto consecrated Abbey territory.

'Miss Ferguson's taste in clothes remains unfathomable,' sighed one

fashion commentator, somewhat despairingly, in June. In no department of Sarah's wardrobe was this more apparent than in the choice of her wedding dress. As soon as her engagement became public, everyone seemed to weigh in with predictions about the style of her bridal gown, based on what little was known of her fashion likes and dislikes and upon the assumed prospect that she would have lost anything up to a stone in weight between March and July.

But the battle to anticipate this most closely guarded of royal wedding secrets was soon conceded. Right up to her marriage, Sarah was nothing if not all-embracing in her choice of fashion lines, favouring plain, close-fitting dresses one day, voluminous frilled numbers the next; dullish, sensible suits with over-large, wide hats on one occasion, and crisp, vivid outfits with sophisticated millinery on another. Those who make a living out

of rationalising these matters could not agree whether she needed to lose weight, whether her hair should be shortened, put up or left to tumble about her shoulders. When she chose a hitherto little-known designer, Paul Golding, to produce some twenty-five outfits for her, his notion that 'women should look like women' was taken to mean an end to her slightly tomboy image, while his professed clientèle of 'discerning women with a strong line in common sense, not clothes alcoholics who are forever updating their wardrobes with the latest gimmicks' suggested that he would toe the traditional royal line and design clothes which could be worn over several years, with suitable adjustments if necessary.

But none of this gave anybody any clues about her wedding dress, in which connection it seemed that she had deliberately chosen its designer, Lindka

"What? Can't hear you!" shouted Sarah and Andrew (right) to thousands of wellwishers calling for an encore of an earlier kiss (above). It was a moment of fun in a brief balcony appearence by them, and members of both families (previous pages). Overleaf: the official group portrait included forty-seven royals and in-laws.

Cierach – another comparative unknown – in order to keep the pundits guessing. Sarah's choice of Miss Cierach was rumbled ten days before Buckingham Palace made the announcement, which allowed enough time to discover that she had already designed ballgowns for the Duchess of Kent, Queen Anne-Marie of the Hellenes and the Duchess of Westminster, as well as wedding dresses for Lady Rose Cecil, a daughter of Lord

Salisbury, Pandora Stevens, and Charlotte Monckton, one of Britain's richest heiresses. What was more, she was at that very time at work on Carolyn Beckwith-Smith's wedding gown, and it was Carolyn in fact who had suggested Lindka to Sarah. 'She is absolutely brilliant,' Carolyn said later. 'You will go along to her with your own ideas, and she will quickly tell you what will work and what will not.'

As Sarah's wedding dress proved, Lindka justified her reputation for being a perfectionist who devotes minute attention to detail. For an artist dedicated to pearls and sequins, she did not overplay her hand, while the combination of fundamental simplicity of design and flourishes of regality in concept supported the catchy tag that a colleague had invested her with – not a high fashion designer, but a creator of highly desirable dresses.

The dress, made from pure silk produced at the Lullingstone silk farm near Sherbourne in Dorset, and an entrancingly feminine contrast to the sober trappings of Andrew's naval

PHONE HOME

A classic for the family album (opposite): Andrew and Sarah with their four pages and four bridesmaids after the ceremony. And a touch of family mischief, fast becoming traditional, means that a teddy-bear goes on honeymoon (above) along with a reminder to keep in touch (left). The L-plate below the carriage really was caddish!

uniform, was complemented by those worn by her bridesmaids. Unlike Princess Diana before her, Sarah chose very young bridesmaids. The oldest, seven-year-old Lady Rosanagh Innes-Ker, is the daughter of the Duke of Roxburghe at whose Scottish residence, Floors Castle, Andrew proposed to Sarah. The other three bridesmaids are all related to either bride or groom: Alice Ferguson is Sarah's half-sister, Laura Fellowes is Princess Diana's niece, and Zara Phillips is Princess Anne's only daughter. Zara's eight-year-old brother Peter was among the four pages, along with Prince William, Andrew Ferguson (Sarah's half-brother) and Seamus Makim (her nephew). Keeping the whole of this young troupe of scene-stealers in some kind of order was the task assigned to Prince Edward – at least when he wasn't acting as Andrew's best man, or supporter, as a royal best man is usually termed.

The choice of bridesmaids, pages and supporter is one of the many reminders that, for all that a royal wedding is anticipated, watched and analysed – as this one was – by hundreds of millions of people around the world, it is essentially a family occasion, and the almost intimate beginning of a new life for two young people in particular. For Prince Andrew, the changes he now faces are personal, and he is well used to having to adapt personally to circumstances. But for Sarah there are public changes to be encountered and coped with. The fact that the critics and the republicans kept their grumbles to themselves during those first four formative months does not mean that it will always be so. She faces a lifetime's scrutiny by a public that insists on the best when it comes to service from its Royal Family. She must expect, sadly, to be spied upon and commented upon, no matter how trivial or how serious the issue, by all manner of folk who should know better or who cannot be expected to know better. If her new sisters-in-law, Princesses Anne and Diana, were asked for advice, they would

both insist that you must learn to live with the consequences of being or becoming public property, no matter how tough the going gets. And if the going gets really tough, Sarah will do well to remember the motto she chose to accompany her new coat-of-arms. It says simply: *Ex Adversis Felicitas Crescit* – Out of Adversity, Happiness Grows. She's had her fair share of adversity and has survived it to become one of the most obviously happy and carefree royals we have. That augurs well for the future.

Two of the superb formal photographs (above & far left) chosen personally by the Queen to mark the Duke and Duchess of York's wedding. Both were taken by American photographer Albert Watson in the Throne Room of Buckingham Palace. (Opposite) The other extreme: a giant-sized teddy bear accompanies Andrew and a windblown Sarah on their last carriage ride of the day — the two-mile drive to Chelsea where a helicopter awaited to take them on honeymoon.